Text Classics

LESBIA VENNER KEOGH was born in Brighton, Melbourne, in 1891, the eldest child of a wealthy financial-agent father and a mother of aristocratic descent. A debilitating heart condition saw her suffer ill health from birth. The family's fortunes turned by the early twentieth century; Lesbia's father moved to Western Australia to work as a labourer, leaving his wife with four young children and little means.

Lesbia attended convent schools in Melbourne and Ballarat before giving up her Catholic faith. She enrolled at the University of Melbourne in 1912, funding her own studies, and completed a law degree four years later in the same graduating class as Robert Menzies. While a student she became involved in radical politics, campaigning against the war and conscription. Her concern for the plight of workers saw her take a position, after graduation, in a clothing factory.

At university she had also met the political activist Guido Baracchi and the philosophy lecturer Katie Lush: her relationships with both would last the rest of her life. In 1920, though, she married Patrick Harford, an artist and like her an Industrial Workers of the World member. The marriage was short-lived, and Lesbia moved back in with her mother. She returned to law and became an articled clerk. In declining health after contracting tuberculosis, she died in 1927.

Lesbia Harford published few poems in her lifetime. When her first appeared in 1921, she had been filling notebooks with verse for at least a decade. Her work, gathered in posthumous collections and various anthologies, has since been acclaimed for its clear and unadorned style. A rediscovered novel, *The Invaluable Mystery*, was published in 1987.

GERALD MURNANE was born in Melbourne in 1939. He has been a primary teacher, an editor and a university lecturer. His debut novel, *Tamarisk Row* (1974), was followed by ten other works of fiction, including *The Plains* and most recently *Border Districts*. *Green Shadows and Other Poems* was published in 2019 and *Last Letter to a Reader* in 2021. In 1999 Murnane won the Patrick White Award and in 2009 he won the Melbourne Prize for Literature. He lives in western Victoria.

ALSO BY LESBIA HARFORD

Collected Poems
The Invaluable Mystery

Selected Poems
Lesbia Harford

Text Publishing Melbourne Australia

The Text Publishing Company acknowledges the Traditional Owners of the country on which we work, the Wurundjeri people of the Kulin Nation, and pays respect to their Elders past and present.

textpublishing.com.au

The Text Publishing Company

Wurundjeri Country, Level 6, Royal Bank Chambers, 287 Collins Street, Melbourne Victoria 3000 Australia

Published by The Text Publishing Company, 2023

Cover image and design by W. H. Chong
Page design by Text
Typeset in Sabon LT Pro 11/16pt by Text

Printed and bound in Australia by Griffin Press, an accredited ISO/NZS 14001:2004 Environmental Management System printer.

ISBN: 9781922790293 (paperback)
ISBN: 9781922791399 (ebook)

A catalogue record for this book is available from the National Library of Australia.

CONTENTS

The Ideal Reader
by Gerald Murnane

NEARLY thirty years have passed since I took my last class as a teacher of fiction writing at tertiary level. I was employed as such a teacher for sixteen years, and during that time I presided over more than two thousand classes. (I'm trying to avoid reporting that I actually *taught* fiction writing. I certainly helped many people to write better fiction but I doubt whether I taught anyone who had never attempted fiction how to write the stuff that we call by that name.)

During class discussions, I spent much time in suggesting improvements to pieces submitted for assessment—turning non-sentences into sentences, changing the order of the phrases or clauses in a sentence, or removing needless words—but sometimes, during a private conference with an outstanding student writer, I would pose questions that I myself could not readily answer: what are we actually doing when we're writing what we call fiction; and for what purpose are we doing it?

Some of my own books had been published by then, but I still pondered these questions. My books had been accepted as fiction, but I was uneasy. I had never quite put behind me the simple-minded dictum of my schooldays: fiction reports the words, thoughts and deeds of imaginary persons who resemble actual persons, thereby expanding our knowledge of human nature. (Not only my teachers and the authors of my school textbooks seemed to believe this. Generations of reviewers and commentators seem never to have questioned it.) In my teens, when I first dreamed of writing for publication, I considered myself utterly unqualified to attempt fiction, so ignorant was I of human nature. I seemed qualified to attempt only the sort of poetry in which a solitary or outcast figure tries to resolve some or another pressing concern. Yet there was I, three or four decades later, a senior lecturer in fiction writing with a sound working knowledge of his craft, so it seemed, but still in search of a theoretical understanding of it.

On a certain afternoon in the early 1990s, a certain outstanding student and I were discussing the questions mentioned in the second paragraph above. (I've long since forgotten her surname but I still recall a few passages from her fiction—or, rather, I still recall my reaction to those passages.) We had been discussing certain claims made by writers in the *Paris Review* interviews: claims such as that every work of fiction is concerned with the mystery of a personality, and that we read and write fiction in order to overcome our fundamental inability to understand one another. At one point, my collocutor asserted that she refused to give up hope and that she wrote *her* fiction for the *one* reader who might understand why it had been written.

From the very beginning of my career, so to call it, I've felt compelled, when planning a new work of fiction, to consider again my motives and my purposes, and while I've never expected to explain once and for all such complex matters, I've come to rely on that statement by my student of long ago. During the past few decades, I've first acknowledged and then, more recently, named her whose sympathetic acceptance of my books was my chief hope while I was planning and writing them. I call her my Ideal Reader. My being a male requires her to be a female, but I try to avoid speculating as to her appearance or her character or, if she has already been born, her whereabouts. I prefer her to be defined only by her insights into the personage responsible for my writing and, following from those insights, her commensurate sympathy. (I learnt as a child, and I've had it confirmed repeatedly since, that the reading and the writing of fiction are processes far more complex than most readers and writers seem to acknowledge, and my knowing what I know of those processes obliged me to write *personage* rather than *person* in the previous sentence.)

I had no need to call into existence any sort of ideal reader until I began to think of myself as a writer. So far as I can recall, I was reading fiction and poetry for about ten years before I first tried to write either. This being so, my speculations about an ideal *author* must have been well under way before I first felt the need for an ideal reader.

My ideal author, so I hoped, would have written a work of fiction or even a single poem that would reveal to me the sort of person I should strive to become, the sort of landscape I should strive to inhabit, and the sort of female person who should accompany me thither. These were the hopes of a mere child, of course, but they serve as evidence for my lifelong reliance on fictional texts to teach me what another sort of man might have sought to learn from actuality, as some would call it.

When, in my fourth decade, I became myself a published author of fiction, I felt still in need of an ideal author, but he was now an older, wiser colleague rather than a father or uncle. He was a male, of course. Only a male, so I believed, could be the hero and exemplar and teacher that I needed. Only a male author, so I believed, could have had to struggle, as I seemed always obliged to struggle, before he was able to complete a publishable work and could have been driven, while he struggled, to envisage a sympathetic but demanding female reader. In the years when I was still hesitant and unpublished, my search for an ideal author seemed sometimes so urgent that I would read the biography of some or another candidate when I might have been better occupied working on my own sentences and paragraphs. Not surprisingly, I never discovered my long-sought mentor, and after the publication of my first few books a version of him survived only as a personage in my private mythology, while a version of myself seemed to have become for a few readers a personage of worth.

I may have given up long ago my search for an exemplary personage to be found on the far side of some or another text, but my need for the other sort of personage became only more urgent with time and her presence was never to be doubted. Merely to conceive of a fictional project was to call her into existence, however remote and shadowy, and many of the decisions that I had to make while I brought the project into being were resolved by my deciding what might and what might not be worthy of her approval.

One other matter has to be reported before I first mention the female person named on the cover of this book or the personage to whom I attribute the poems on the pages within it. From my early teens until my mid-thirties, I wrote perhaps a hundred poems. Three were actually published in obscure organs; perhaps a dozen were sent to respected literary periodicals and later returned to me unwanted; all have rested for nearly fifty years in a drawer labelled POETRY in my so-called Literary Archive. During that time, of course, I became known as an author of prose fiction, and I wondered not infrequently why I had seemingly succeeded in one sort of writing but had seemingly failed in another sort. Occasionally, I looked at some of the poems, hoping to resolve my uncertainty, but I could not begin to assess them as an editor or a publisher might have done, and my experience as a published writer had taught me that those worthies arrived at most of their decisions after having sniffed what I called the winds of fashion.

Never mind the date on the calendar—I knew the day only as Cox Plate Day, the Saturday between Caulfield Cup Day and Victoria Derby Day. On Cox Plate Day in 2014 I was leafing through the literary pages of the *Australian*, hoping that no review would seem worth reading and that I could spend the rest of my morning coffee break with the *Herald Sun* form guide. I have no need to rely on my memory of that notable morning. I retrieved just now from my Chronological Archive the review that I read of *Collected Poems*, by Lesbia Harford, and the comment that I wrote soon afterwards. I wrote:

> Soon after I had read the attached item in today's *Australian* and had fallen in love with Lesbia Harford, I sent a note to my bookseller, asking him to get me a copy of the book under review. Soon afterwards, again, I wrote a poem that can be found in the drawer labelled POETRY in the Literary Archive. Soon afterwards, again, I made notes for another poem and resolved to finish at least four lines of poetry every day in future.

I doubt whether I kept to that last resolution, but six months later I had written the final drafts of almost every one of the poems in my collection, *Green Shadows and Other Poems*, which was published in 2019. Forty and more years before, I had struggled for evening after evening to produce a few barely satisfying lines, but in the summer of my seventy-fifth year I heard line after fluent line arranging itself whenever I was alone. More than once, I stopped by the roadside in some vast, empty landscape in western Victoria, where I live, and scribbled on the notepad kept in my glovebox the lines or the whole stanza that had come to me almost unbidden during the previous ten minutes.

What had happened to me? My preferred answer is to declare that I had discovered at last not only the two ideal personages that I had glimpsed for decades past but the one personage who embodied them both.

> Pat wasn't Pat last night at all.
> He was the rain—
> The Spring—
> Young Dionysus white and warm—
> Lilac and everything.

I had been reading the review with mild interest until I came to these five lines: an islet of poetry in an expanse of white blankness among paragraphs of undistinguished prose. What I noted at first was that the five lines were, in fact, poetry. For much of my life, I had privately refused to accept as poetry most of what my contemporaries called by that name. For my own satisfaction, I had sometimes transcribed a piece by someone praised as a poet and had been confirmed in my suspicion that the writing was no more than a body of faulty, jarring prose arranged in lines of arbitrary length with inaccurate or inadequate punctuation marks. For much of my life, my need for poetry was satisfied by earlier, traditional works or, after I had learnt Hungarian in middle age, by the wealth of lyric poetry in that melodious language, with its abundant rhymes and alliterative possibilities.

The impact on me of the whole of the brief poem was instant and powerful. What I'm writing now is my analysis of the causes of that impact. I was surely aware of what I would call the quiet rhymes and the muted half-rhyme. Even more to my liking would have been the pattern of stresses: four in the first line followed by two, one, four and three in the remaining lines. Now, this pattern can surely not be called regular, and yet I found it fully satisfying in the way that a traditional stanza is satisfying or a folk song arrives at its fore-ordained ending. And when I tried to account for this, I remembered Gerard Manley Hopkins.

I was introduced to Hopkins' poetry in 1955 by the only competent teacher from my schooldays, and so began my lifelong interest in the workings of rhythm—not just in poetry but also in prose and even in what Robert Frost called the sound of sense, meaning one's interpretation of a conversation heard from a distance as mere sounds. (My preferred example is the gradual crescendo and the subsequent sudden falling away of the call of a horse race from a distant radio on many a Saturday afternoon in my childhood.) I used the word *satisfying* in the previous paragraph, but I might have used a stronger word. A rhythm such as that in the quoted poem compels me often to recite the lines aloud more than once for the pleasure to be got from my sense of the rightness of the whole.

The rhythm was not even the half of it. However satisfying might be the sound of a word or its positioning in a pattern of stresses, its denotation matters far more to me and, surely, to any thoughtful reader. But, as I reported earlier, reading poetry or fiction is for me a hugely complicated process. Since my early childhood, I've sought to get from the reading and the writing of poetry and fiction more than I've expected to get from any other experience, and my lifelong search has made me very much alert to connotations.

The word *lilac* leapt at me when I first read it. I saw in mind immediately a certain shade or colour. Next, I saw a certain flower, smallish and arranged in a cluster. What I did *not* experience was a memory of any sort of odour. This was because I was born without a sense of smell. I've never smelled a lilac or any other flower or anything else said to have an odour. I should add that I've never regarded this as any sort of deprivation. Shut out of the world of smells and odours, I seem to have developed an unusually keen awareness of colours and their countless variations. I can recall, for example, the precise shade of the clusters of blooms that appeared every October on the tall shrub under which I built my first pretend racecourse nearly eighty years ago, which shrub was an uncommon variety of lilac, and the sight of that or any other shade of lilac, or of any printed mention of the lilac plant, gives rise unfailingly to a wealth of valued associations. So it was with the word *lilac* in Harford's poem on the sunny October morning of Cox Plate Day nearly nine years ago. But the appearance close by of the word *white* set in motion such a process as I've often experienced but have written about only in fictional contexts.

One of the central landscapes of my private mythology might be called, for convenience, the Western District of Victoria. My landscape only faintly resembles an actual district of that name, although the resemblance was rather more apparent a century ago. One of the several means by which I discovered my landscape was my poring over, as a child, the pocket-sized race books that my father sometimes brought home from places such as Penshurst, Casterton or Hamilton. I learnt from one of those booklets, about seventy years ago, that an aged gelding named Parentive was owned and trained by a man named A. S. Gartner of Hamilton, whose racing colours comprised a jacket of white and lilac hoops with white sleeves and a white cap. Within hours of my having learnt this information—or, perhaps, within minutes—there had entered, once and for all, into my mythology a host of imagery to do with a man of enviable wealth, of acute discernment, and of reserved demeanour, and to do with the far-reaching and mostly level grassy landscape surrounding the clumps of English trees that concealed for much of the year his family home. (I was for some time unable to find inspiration in the name of the racehorse that carried Mr Gartner's eloquent colours, but only until I was able to infer that the seemingly meaningless name had been derived from the name of the gelding's sire, Parenthesis. This was enough to allow me to feel about my new-found cluster of imagery a confidence that the whole of it was somehow marginal, or bracketed off, as it were, from the world as it was usually understood.)

If any reader of this piece of writing finds it strange as a recommendation for a selection of poetry, I assure that reader that I intend the piece to be the warmest possible recommendation. The poetry or the prose fiction that I most esteem is that which reaches the same part of me that has driven me for most of my life to write my own sort of writing. A biographer of Marcel Proust praised him for having conveyed to his readers the scent of invisible yet enduring lilacs. Such was my mood while I was reading again recently the best of Harford's poems that I dared to suppose that Mr A. S. Gartner may have put the lilac into his unforgettable racing colours after he had read, on afternoon after tranquil afternoon in his upper-storey library with its windows shaded by English trees, the biography just mentioned, or even the far-reaching masterpiece of Proust himself.

~

The collected edition that I read in 2014 included 245 poems. I was asked by the publishers of this edition to select no more than eighty. I selected exactly eighty. I arrived at this total more by rejecting than by selecting. I first rejected most of the poems in which were the words *beauty, beautiful, lovely, fair,* or *love* used as a noun. I rejected also some poems in which the word *love* seemed used too often as a verb. (Proust's narrator wrote of his preference for writing not 'I loved Albertine' but such as 'I felt the desire to kiss Albertine'.) From the many poems remaining after these processes of rejection, I selected those that caused me, if only slightly, to change my view of things: that opened my eyes more widely or refined my vision or begged me to review my preferences and prejudices.

I confess, finally, to having rejected many of the poems in which the poet makes mention of a husband or a male lover. The ideal can have its roots only in the actual, and to love an ideal writer/reader is not to be free from actual jealousy.

SELECTED POEMS

'I DREAMT LAST NIGHT'

I dreamt last night
That spring had come.
Across green fields I saw a blur
Of crimson-blossomed plum.

I've never known
So fair a thing.
And yet I wish it were a dream
Of some forgotten spring.

Today the sun
Our workroom blest
And there was hard young wattle pinned
On our forewoman's breast.

'AY, AY, AY, THE LILIES OF THE GARDEN'

Ay, ay, ay, the lilies of the garden
With red threads binding them and stars about,
These shall be her symbols, for she is high and holy,
Holy in her maidenhood and very full of doubt.

Ay, ay, ay, for she is very girlish,
Fearful her heart's lilies should be stained by sin.
Yet will I bind them with rosy threads of passion.
Surely human passion has a right to enter in.

'I COUNT THE DAYS UNTIL
I SEE YOU, DEAR'

I count the days until I see you, dear,
But the days only.
I dare not reckon up the nights and hours
I shall be lonely.

But when at last I meet you, dearest heart,
How can it cheer me?
Desire has power to turn me into stone,
When you come near me.

I give my heart the lie against my will,
Seem not to see you,
Glance aside quickly if I meet your eye,
Love you and flee you.

'SOME HAPPY PEOPLE CAN SEE AND HEAR HIM DAILY'

Some happy people can see and hear him daily,
Chosen friends and trusted. Would that I were one.
I can only think of him and long for him and love him,
Love him from the rising to the setting of the sun.

Some happy people can spend the evenings with him.
Softly must the hours step when the gold stars shine.
I can only think of him and long for him and love him.
Plotting still and planning still to make such moments
    mine.

THE TROOP-SHIPS

Up the river in the sun,
We rowed slowly.
Oftentimes the willow boughs
Screened us wholly.
Ours were all the tiny joys
That bless the lowly.

Mighty ships upon the seas
Onward bore you.
Battles dim and agony
Lay before you.
I half-wished our willows spread
Their branches o'er you.

I can't feel the sunshine
Or see the stars aright
For thinking of her beauty
And her kisses bright.

She would let me kiss her
Once and not again.
Deeming soul essential,
Sense doth she disdain.

If I should once kiss her,
I would never rest
Till I had lain hour long
Pillowed on her breast.

Lying so, I'd tell her
Many a secret thing
God has whispered to me
When my soul took wing.

Would that I were Sappho,
Greece my land, not this!
There the noblest women,
When they loved, would kiss.

AFTER RAIN

Today
I'd like to be a nun
And go and say
My rosary beneath the trees out there.
In this shy sun
The raindrops look like silver beads of prayer.

So blest
Am I, I'd like to tell
God and the rest
Of heaven-dwellers in the garden there
All that befell
Last week. Such gossip is as good as prayer.

Ah well!
I have, since I'm no nun,
No beads to tell,
And being happy must be all my prayer.
Yet 'twould be fun
To walk with God 'neath the wet trees out there.

SUMMER LIGHTNING

Just now, as warm day faded from our sight,
Hosts of archangels, fleet
On lightning-wingèd feet
Passed by, all glimmering in the busy night.

Sweet angels, bring no blinding truth to birth,
Give us no messages
From heavenly palaces;
Leave us our dark trees and our starlight earth.

BIRTHDAY

I have a sister whom God gave to me;
He formed her out of trouble and the mists of the sea.

Like Aphrodite, she came to me full-grown.
Oh, I am blest forever with a sister of my own.

Can I not keep you alive,
Must you go roaming
Further than I can follow,
O bee with a star for a hive?
All your flight's but a homing
Sunward, my swallow.

NOLI ME TANGERE

We watched the dawn breaking across the sea
While just above us hung the evening star.
The nearer waters took a hint of white
And clouds and waves together massed afar,
Narrowed our morning world of pallid light
Till dawn seemed very close to you and me.

'Nay, dawn, stay farther off. Be Magdalen.
Go back into the distance whence you came.
The Near is meaningless when Far is nought,'
So I; and you, 'Wait but a little then,
And day, whole day, uprising like a flame,
Will show us the far reaches of our thought.'

They say—priests say—
That God loves the world.
Maybe he does,
When the dew is pearl'd
On the emerald grass,
Or the young dawns shine.
Would you be satisfied,
Proteus mine,
Just to be loved
When your hair was curled,
As Earth is beloved
When Earth is fine?
I love you more
Than God loves the world.

My mission in the world
Is to prolong
Rapture, by turning it
Into a song.

A song of liberty
Bound by no rule!
No marble meaning's mine
Fixed for a school.

My singing ecstasy
Winged for the flight,
Each will hear differently,
And hear aright.

Today they made a bonfire
Close to the cherry tree
And smoke like incense drifted
Through the white tracery.

I think the gardener really
Played a tremendous game,
Offering beauty homage
In soft blue smoke and flame.

'OURS WAS A FRIENDSHIP IN SECRET, MY DEAR'

Ours was a friendship in secret, my dear,
Stolen from fate.
I must be secret still, show myself calm
Early and late.

'Isn't it sad he was killed!' I must hear
With a smooth face.
'Yes, it is sad.'—Oh, my darling, my own,
My heart of grace.

'THE HOT WINDS WAKE TO LIFE IN THE SWEET DAYTIME'

The hot winds wake to life in the sweet daytime
My weary limbs,
And tear through all the moonlit darkness shouting
Tremendous hymns.

My body keeps earth's law and goes exulting.
Poor slavish thing!
The soul that knows you dead rejects in silence
This riotous spring.

Somebody brought in lilac—
Lilac after rain.
Isn't it strange, belovèd of mine,
You'll not see it again?

Lilac glad with the sun on it
Flagrant fair from birth,
Mourns in colour, belovèd of mine,
You laid in the earth.

When I am making poetry I'm good
And happy then.
I live in a deep world of angelhood
Afar from men.
And all the great and bright and fiery troop
Kiss me agen
With love. Deathless Ideas! I have no need
Of girls' lips then.

Goodness and happiness and poetry,
I put them by.
I will not rush with great wings gloriously
Against the sky
While poor men sit in holes, unbeautiful,
Unsouled, and die.
Better let misery and pettiness
Make me their sty.

There's a little boy who lives next door
With hair like you—
Pale, pale hair and a rose-white skin
And his eyes are blue.

When I get a chance I peep at him,
Who is so like you—
Terribly like, my dead, my fair,
For he's dumb too.

'HOW ARE THE HOURS EMPLOYED
I SPEND WITH YOU'

How are the hours employed I spend with you—
In talk of incidents that fill the soul
As much and little as such trifles do?

Nay, we are busied with great books, where fears
On lightning certainties like thunder roll
In conflict elemental through the years.

The man who painted this is dead today
As Leslie is—and yet how differently!
He left great pictures for the world to see
While Leslie left an image in one heart,
One only heart that may inconstant prove.
O heart, be strong and let the gazers know
There is no beauty like enduring love.

I do hate the folk I love,
They hurt so.
Their least word and act may be
Source of woe.

'Won't you come to tea with me?'
'Not today.
I'm so tired, I've been to church,'
Such folk say.

All the dreary afternoon
I must clutch
At the strength to love like them—
Not too much.

All that I scribble
Her eyes must see,
Who rends the body
And soul of me.

What might I scribble
If she weren't there?
Many a secret
Would I lay bare.

Then might she wonder
That love and hate,
Irreconcilable,
Yet can mate.

I think her selfish
And cold and hard—
Give her black titles
That stretch a yard.

Yet in a minute
My breath is spent,
Swearing her noble
And innocent.

Must love be feeble
Where hate is set?
Loving or hating,
I can't forget.

'ALL DAY LONG'

All day long
We sew fine muslin up for you to wear,
Muslin that women wove for you elsewhere,
A million strong.

Just like flames,
Insatiable, you eat up all our hours
And sun and loves and tea and talk and flowers,
Suburban dames.

THE IMMIGRANT

When Gertie came in
To work today
She was much less weary
And far more gay.

We asked her the reason
Of this delight.
She had been dreaming
Of home all night.

Green and blue
First-named of colours believe these two.
They first of colours by men were seen
This grass colour, tree colour,
Sky colour, sea colour,
Magic-named, mystic-souled, blue and green.

Later came
Small subtle colours like tongues of flame,
Small jewel colours for treasure trove,
Not fruit colour, flower colour,
Cloud colour, shower colour,
But purple, amethyst, violet and mauve.

These remain,
Two broad fair colours for our larger gain
Stretched underfoot or spreading wide on high,
Green beech colour, vine colour,
Gum colour, pine colour,
Blue of the noonday and the moonlit sky.

FATHERLESS

I've had no man
To guard and shelter me,
Guide and instruct me
From mine infancy.

No lord of earth
To show me day by day
What things a girl should do
And what she should say.

I have gone free
Of manly excellence
And hold their wisdom
More than half pretence.

For since no male
Has ruled me or has fed,
I think my own thoughts
In my woman's head.

WORK-GIRL'S HOLIDAY

A lady has a thousand ways
Of doing nothing all her days,
And so she thinks that they're well spent;
She can be idle and content.
But when I have a holiday
I have forgotten how to play.

I could rest idly under trees
When there's some sun and little breeze
Or if the wind should prove too strong
Could lie in bed the whole day long.
But any leisured girl would say
That that was waste of holiday.

Perhaps if I had weeks to spend
In doing nothing without end,
I might learn better how to shirk
And never want to go to work.

Each day I sit in an ill-lighted room
To teach a boy.
For one hour by the clock great words and dreams
Are our employ.

We read St Agnes' Eve and that more fair
Eve of St Mark
At a small table up against the wall
In the half-dark.

I tell him all the wise things I have read
Concerning Keats.
'His earlier work is overfull of sense
And sensual sweets.'

I tell him all that comes into my mind
From God-knows-where,
Remark, 'In English poets Bertha's type
Is jolly rare.

She's a real girl that strains her eyes to read
And cricks her neck.
Now Madeline could pray all night nor feel
Her body's check.

And Bertha *reads*—p'rhaps the first reading girl
In English rhyme.'
It's maddening work to say what Keats has said
A second time.

The boy sits sideways with averted head.
His brown cheek glows.
I like his black eyes and his sprawling limbs
And his short nose.

He, feeling, dreads the splendour of the verse,
But he must learn
To write about it neatly and to quote
These lines that burn.

He drapes his soul in my obscuring words,
Makes himself fit
To go into a sunny world and take
His part in it.

'Examiners' point of view, you know,' say I,
'Is commonsense.
You must sift poetry before you can
Sift Evidence.'

MACHINISTS TALKING

I sit at my machine
Hourlong beside me, Vera, aged nineteen,
Babbles her sweet and innocent tale of sex.

Her boy, she hopes, will prove
Unlike his father in the act of love.
Twelve children are too many for her taste.

She looks sidelong, blue-eyed,
And tells a girlish story of a bride
With the sweet licence of Arabian queens.

Her child, she says, saw light
Minute for minute, nine months from the night
The mother first lay in her lover's arms.

She says a friend of hers
Is a man's mistress who gives jewels and furs
But will not have her soft limbs cased in stays.

I open my small store
And tell of a young delicate girl, a whore,
Stole from her mother many months ago.

Fate made the woman seem
To have a tiger's loveliness, to gleam
Strong and fantastic as a beast of prey.

I sit at my machine.
Hourlong beside me, Vera, aged nineteen,
Babbles her sweet and innocent tale of sex.

THE INVISIBLE PEOPLE

When I go into town at half past seven
Great crowds of people stream across the ways,
Hurrying, although it's only half past seven.
They are the invisible people of the days.

When you go in to town about eleven
The hurrying, morning crowds are hid from view.
Shut in the silent buildings at eleven
They toil to make life meaningless for you.

CLOSING TIME: PUBLIC LIBRARY

At ten o'clock the great gong sounds its dread
Prelude to splendour. I push back my chair,
And all the people leave their books. We flock,
Still acquiescent, down the marble stair
Into the dark where we can't read. And thought
Swoops down insatiate through the starry air.

THE TWO SWANS

There's a big park just close to where we live—
Trees in a row
And shaggy grass whereon the dead leaves blow.

And in the middle round a great lagoon
The fair yachts sail
In loveliness that makes the water pale.

Last night I went to walk along the road
Beside the park
And feel the kisses of the wintry dark.

It's the best place to watch the evening come,
For mists are there
And lights and shadows and the lake is fair.

And last night looking up I saw two swans
Fly overhead
With long black necks and their white wings
     outspread.

Above the houses citywards they went,
An arrowy pair
In secret—white and black and dark and fair.

'I WAS SAD'

I was sad
Having signed up in a rebel band,
Having signed up to rid the land
Of a plague it had.

For I knew
That I would suffer, I would be lost,
Be bitter and foolish and tempest tost
And a failure too.

I was sad;
Though far in the future our light would shine,
For the present the dark was ours, was mine.
I couldn't be glad.

'MY LOVELY PIXIE, MY GOOD COMPANION'

My lovely pixie, my good companion,
You do not love me, bed-mate of mine,
Save as a child loves—
Careless of loving,
Rather preferring raspberry wine.

How can you help it? You were abandoned.
Your mother left you. Your father died.
All your young years of
Pain and desertion
Are not forgotten, here at my side.

'INTO OLD RHYME'

Into old rhyme
The new words come but shyly.
Here's a brave man
Who sings of commerce dryly.

Swift-gliding cars
Through town and country winging,
Like cigarettes,
Are deemed unfit for singing.

Into old rhyme
New words come tripping slowly.
Hail to the time
When they possess it wholly.

Now I've been three days
In the place where I am staying,
I've taken up new ways—
Landowning and flute playing.

There's an orchard ground
Seen, that set me sighing.
Should I give ten pounds,
It is mine for buying.

With the door set wide
I could sit there playing,
Send the magic notes
Through the gully straying.

Since the roof is sound
And the trees are growing,
I will give ten pounds,
All my gold bestowing.

Now I've been three days
In the place where I am staying,
I've taken up new ways—
· Landowning and flute playing.

'I FOUND AN ORCHID IN THE VALLEY FAIR'

I found an orchid in the valley fair,
And named it for us both,
And left it there.

Two flowers upon one stem, white-souled, alone—
I couldn't pull them up,
And bring them home.

'FLORENCE KNEELS DOWN TO SAY HER PRAYERS'

Florence kneels down to say her prayers
At night.
I wonder what she says and why she cares
To pray at night.

I think when she kneels down to pray
At night
The names that have been on her lips all day
Are there, at night.

She interferes with destinies
At night.
My loves are free to do the things they please
By day, or night.

I like the riders
Clad in rose and blue,
Their colours glitter
And their horses too.

Swift go the riders
On incarnate speed.
My thought can scarcely
Follow where they lead.

Delicate, strong, long
Lines of colour flow,
And all the people
Tremble as they go.

'THERE IS A CHILD'S NAME THAT I WANT TO SAY'

There is a child's name that I want to say
Though the child lives ten thousand miles away
And I've no notion what his name may be.
It is some strange wild word of Hungary.

And I've no way of knowing if he brooks
To bear his father's image in his looks.
But he is beautiful. There's none above him.
He is my lover's son and so I love him.

'I AM AFRAID'

I am afraid
He'll someday stop loving me.
All of them say
He'll someday stop loving me—
That's how he's made.

If I upbraid
And say he'll stop loving me
He always swears
He'll never stop loving me.
But I'm afraid.

'I'M LIKE ALL LOVERS, WANTING
LOVE TO BE'

I'm like all lovers, wanting love to be
A very mighty thing for you and me.

In certain moods your love should be a fire
That burnt your very life up in desire.

The only kind of love then to my mind
Would make you kiss my shadow on the blind

And walk seven miles each night to see it there
Myself within, serene and unaware.

But you're as bad. You'd have me watch the clock
And count your coming while I mend your sock.

You'd have my mind devoted day and night
To you and care for you and your delight.

Poor fools, who each would have the other give
What spirit must withhold if it would live.

You're not my slave, I wish you not to be.
I love yourself and not your love for me,

The self that goes Ten thousand miles away
And loses thought of me for many a day.

And you loved me for loving much beside
But now you want a woman for your bride.

Oh, make no woman of me, you who can,
Or I will make a husband of a man.

By my unwomanly love that sets you free
Love all myself, but least the woman in me.

BUDDHA IN THE WORKROOM

Sometimes the skirts I push through my machine
Spread circlewise, strong-petalled lobe on lobe,
And look for the rapt moment of a dream
Like Buddha's robe.

And I, caught up out of the workroom's stir
Into the silence of a different scheme,
Dream, in a sun-dark, templed otherwhere,
His alien dream.

'I HAVE TO MAKE A SOUL
FOR ONE'

I have to make a soul for one
Who lost his soul in childhood's hour.
And I'm not sure—not really sure—
If I have power.

I don't know whether souls are made
With laughter or with faith or pain
But though I fail a thousand times
I'll try again.

A BLOUSE MACHINIST

Miss Murphy has blue eyes and blue-black hair,
Her machine's opposite mine
So I can stare
At her pale face and shining blue-black hair.

I'm sure that other people think her plain
But I could look at her
And look again
Although I see why people think her plain.

She's nice to watch when her machine-belt breaks.
She has such delicate hands
And arms, it takes
Ages for her to mend it when it breaks.

Oh, beauty's still elusive and she's fine.
Though all the moulding
Of her face—the line
Of nose, mouth, chin—is Mongol, yet she's fine.

Of course things would be different in Japan.
They'd see her beauty.
On a silken fan
They'd paint her for a princess in Japan.

But still her loveliness eludes the blind.
They never use their eyes
But just their mind.
So must much loveliness elude the blind.

AN IMPROVER

Maisie's been holding down her head all day,
Her little red head. And her pointed chin
Rests on her neck that slips so softly in
The square-cut low-necked darling dress she made
In such a way, since it's high-waisted too,
It lets you guess how fair young breasts begin
Under the gentle pleasant folds of blue.

But on the roof at lunchtime when the sun
Shone warmly and the wind was blowing free
She lifted up her head to let me see
A little rosy mark beneath her chin—
The mark of kisses. If her mother knew
She'd be ashamed, but a girl-friend like me
Made her feel proud to show her kisses to.

This is a pretty road
With lamps a-swinging
And all along the way
Motor cars winging.

There are wires overhead
Like webs of spiders
And underneath them go
A million riders.

Under this tracery
Where trams go speeding
Seaward or cityward
The road is leading.

You want a lily
And you plead with me
'Give me my lily back.'

I went to see
A friend last night and on her mantelshelf
I saw some lilies,
Image of myself,
And most unlike your dream of purity.

They had been small green lilies, never white
For man's delight
In their most blissful hours.
But now the flowers
Had shrivelled and instead
Shone spikes of seeds,
Burned spikes of seeds,
Burned red
As love and death and fierce futurity.

There's this much of the lily left in me.

Pink eucalyptus flowers
(The flowers are out)
Are scented honey sweet
For bees to buzz about.

Pink eucalyptus flowers
(The flowers are out)
Are fair as any rose
For us to sing about.

'TO LOOK ACROSS AT MOIRA GIVES ME PLEASURE'

To look across at Moira gives me pleasure.
She has a red tape measure.

Her dress is black and all the workroom's dreary,
And I am weary.

But that's like blood—like a thin blood stream
    trickling—
Like a fire quickening.

It's Revolution. *Ohé*, I take pleasure
In Moira's red tape measure.

'I DREAMT LAST NIGHT OF HAPPY HOME-COMINGS'

I dreamt last night of happy home-comings.
Friends I had loved and had believed were dead
Came happily to visit me and said
I was a part of their fair home-coming.

It's strange that I should dream of welcomings
And happy meetings when my love, last week
Returned from exile, did not even speak
Or write to me or need my welcoming.

'HE LOOKS IN MY HEART AND THE IMAGE THERE'

He looks in my heart and the image there
Is himself, himself, than himself more fair.

And he thinks of my heart as a mirror clear
To reflect the image I hold most dear.

But my heart is much more like a stream, I think,
Where my lover may come when he needs to drink.

And my heart is a stream that seems asleep
But the tranquil waters run strong and deep;

They reflect the image that seems most fair
But their meaning and purpose are otherwhere.

He may come, my lover, and lie on the brink
And gaze at his image and smile and drink

While the hidden waters run strong and free,
Unheeded, unguessed at, the soul of me.

My window pane is broken
Just a bit
Where the small curtain doesn't
Cover it.

And in the afternoon
I like to lie
And watch the pepper tree
Against the sky.

Pink berries and blue sky
And leaves and sun
Are very fair to rest
One's eyes upon.

And my tired feet are resting
On the bed
And there's a pillow under
My tired head.

Parties and balls and books
I know are best
But when I've finished work
I like to rest.

'SOMETIMES I THINK THE HAPPIEST OF LOVE'S MOMENTS'

Sometimes I think the happiest of love's moments
Is the blest moment of release from loving.

The world once more is all one's own to model
Upon one's own and not another's pattern.

And each poor heart imprisoned by the other's
Is suddenly set free for splendid action.

For no two lovers are a single person
And lovers' union means a soul's suppression.

Oh, happy then the moment of love's passing
When those strong souls we sought to slay recover.

'THE PEOPLE HAVE DRUNK THE WINE OF PEACE'

The people have drunk the wine of peace
In the streets of town.
They smile as they drift with hearts at rest
Uphill and down.

The people have drunk the wine of peace,
They are mad with joy.
Never again need they lie and fear
Death for a boy.

'I MUST BE DREAMING THROUGH THE DAYS'

I must be dreaming through the days
And see the world with childish eyes
If I'd go singing all my life
And my songs be wise

And in the kitchen or the house
Must wonder at the sights I see.
And I must hear the throb and hum
That moves to song in factory.

So much in life remains unsung,
And so much more than love is sweet.
I'd like a song of kitchenmaids
With steady fingers and swift feet.

And I could sing about the rest
That breaks upon a woman's day
When dinner's over and she lies
Upon her bed to dream and pray

Until the children come from school
And all her evening work begins.
There's more in life than tragic love
And all the storied, splendid sins.

Today, in class,
I read aloud to forty little boys
The legend of King Croesus' boasted joys.

They were so young,
Restless, and eager, I believed they'd find
This moral story little to their mind.

But they were pleased
With the old legend—quick to comprehend
Sorrowful wisdom's triumph at the end:

They seemed to feel,
In hush of wonder, hurry of amaze,
The sure uncertainty of all men's days.

MISS MARY FAIRFAX

Every day Miss Mary goes her rounds
Through the splendid house and through the
    grounds—

Looking if the kitchen table's white—
Seeing that the great big fire's alight—

Finding specks on shining pans and pots—
Never praising much, and scolding lots.

If the table's white, she does not see
Roughened hands that once were ivory.

It is fires, not cheeks, that ought to glow;
And if eyes are dim, she doesn't know.

Blind Miss Mary! Poor for all she owns,
Since the things she loves are stocks and stones.

In this little school
Life goes so sweetly,
Day on azure day
Is lost completely.

No one thinks too much
Or worries greatly.
In a pleasant shade
We dream sedately.

There's no struggle here
Or conflict showing;
Only the sweet pain
Of young limbs growing.

I want this thing and that—
A pudding-bowl, a saucepan,
And a hat
For Pat.

I note some grease—or grime—
A cobweb on the ceiling.
Where's the time
For rhyme?

This being wife
Is not Romance, not Hate, not
'Love to the knife'
But life.

'I HAVE PUT OFF MYSELF
AWHILE'

I have put off myself awhile
And lead another kind of life
Than that where dreams were quickly deeds—
Now I am wife.

But since those days were blessèd days
I've a poor dream about the past.
I'll set it down in words. To words
I fall at last.

I in the library,
Looking for books to read,
Pulled one out twice to see
If it fulfilled my need.

Butler had written this
Autobiography.
Which of the Butlers, then?
I opened it to see.

He's an old general
Mounted upon a horse.
Thinkers don't write their lives,
But soldiers can, of course.

They write: 'The regiment
Was sent to Omdurman,
Where Gordon died. To catch
The Mahdi was our plan.'

Later—'The bride wore white
And she had golden hair.
Four bridesmaids bore her train
Up to the altar where

His Grace of Birmingham'—
It's the old rigmarole,
Names, facts and dates—no word
In this about the soul.

No dreams, no sin, no tears!
Only the body thrives.
Upon such worthless things
Great soldiers base their lives.

No wonder wars are fought.
Loss of such life is small—
Life bound to space and time,
Not infinite at all.

ABOUT TREES

Here, in the Eastern garden's galaxy,
Two song-familiar trees grow side by side:
Arbutus, myrtle; like a mystery
Of maid and bride.

So strong are they, so full of flower and leaf!—
Heine's pale maidens circle in their shade,
And long-forgotten Irish girls of grief
Have hither strayed.

O maiden-haunted trees of Hindustan,
By shadowy fingers are your branches stirred;
And melodies breathe through you softer than
A whispered word.

Sometimes I think God has his days
For being friends.
He says: 'Forgive my careless ways.
No one pretends
I'm always kind; but for today
Do let's be friends.'

And grudgingly I make reply,
'Nice sort of friends.
I think it's time you had a try
To make amends
For things you've done; but after all
Suppose we're friends.'

NEW WINDOW, ST JOHN'S
HAWKSBURN

St John looks up to Christ in the great window
And Christ looks upward to the rose above,
And light streams through upon apostles kneeling—
Victims of glory, sacrificed to love.

Down in the church the pews are out of order.
Workmen climb ladders, seem to risk their lives.
And now and then a party of churchwardens
Enter, accompanied by enquiring wives.

But to the artist, who is keen on colour—
And to the churchfolk, who are rich in pride—
And to the workmen, who must earn their living—
Religion's the excuse. It's nought beside.

'THEY SENT ME PICTURES OF THE SAINTS'

They sent me pictures of the saints
For stained-glass windows. They'll be set
High up in church for all to see:
Mary and Margaret.

Secure in comradeship with God,
Gracious and steadfast, stand they there
Wrapped in long robes of sanctity;
Only their feet are bare.

Ideals at one with the Ideal.
New ciphers in the heavenly code.
Only their naked feet recall
The thorns upon the road.

'A BUNCH OF LILAC AND A STORM OF HAIL'

A bunch of lilac and a storm of hail
On the same afternoon! Indeed I know
Here in the South it always happens so,
That lilac is companioned by the gale.

I took some hailstones from the window sill
And swallowed them in a communion feast.
Their transitory joy is mine at least,
The lilac's loveliness escapes me still.

Mine are the storms of spring, but not the sweets.

Old poets talked
Of the 'eternal hills'
And 'bases of the mountains';
Oh, they walked
And counted steps
And measured dreams out so!
For, unlike these,
The hills I know
Go whirling to and fro
Behind the trees.
Mount Juliet—
On Monday morning set
Above the rest—
At noon or even,
Is with the blest
In heaven.
Not a wraith
Remains to haunt an earthly resting place.
And, lo!
Those golden trees, that strayed

So exquisitely near
An hour ago,
Have wandered off again,
To disappear
In far blue shade.

> *Panton Hills*

'LAST NIGHT, IN A DREAM, I FELT THE PECULIAR ANGUISH'

Last night, in a dream, I felt the peculiar anguish
Known to me of old;
And there passed me, not much changed, my earliest
    lover,
Smiling, suffering, cold.

This morning, I lay with closed lids under the blankets,
Lest with night depart
The truthful dream which restored to me with my
    lover
My passionate heart.

FLOWERS AND LIGHT

Flowers have uncountable ways of pretending to be
Not solid, but moonlight or sunlight or starlight
   with scent.
Primroses strive for the colour of sunshine on lawns
Dew-besprent.

Freesias are flames wherein light more than heat is
   desired,
As candles on altars burn amethyst, golden and white.
Wall-flowers are sun, streaked with shade. Periwinkles
   blue noon
At the height.

A BRONTE LEGEND

They say she was a creature of the moor,
A lover of the angels, silence bound.
She sought no friendships. She was too remote,
Her sister Charlotte found.

I know she nursed her brother till he died,
Although she didn't like him; that she had
Housework and all the ironing to do,
Because her maids were bad.

And in the midst of it she wrote a book
There could have been small leisure for the moor
Or wandering! She used to mend and sew,
The family was so poor.

Her brother died. But she died just as soon
As she had nursed dear Charlotte through the shock
Of Patrick's death. Contemplative? Well, well!—
No Simeon of the Rock!

PRUNING FLOWERING GUMS

One summer day, along the street,
Men pruned the gums
To make them neat.
The tender branches, white with flowers,
Lay in the sun
For hours and hours,
And every hour they grew more sweet—
More honey-like;
Until the street
Smelt like a hive, withouten bees.
But still the gardeners
Lopped the trees.

Then came the children out of school,
Noisy and separate
As their rule
Of being is. The spangled trees
Gave them one heart:
Such power to please
Had all the flowering branches strown

Around for them
To make their own.
Then such a murmuring arose
As made the ears
Confirm the nose
And give the lie to eyes. For hours
Child bees hummed
In the honey flowers.

They gathered sprigs and armfuls. Some
Ran with their fragrant
Burdens home,
And still returned; and after them
Would drag great boughs.
Some stripped a stem
Of rosy flowers and played with these.
Never such love
Had earthly trees
As these young creatures gave. By night,
The treasured sprays
Of their delight
Were garnered every one. The street
Looked, as the council liked it, neat.

'LOVE IS NOT LOVE...'

When I was still a child
I thought my love would be
Noble, truthful, brave,
And very kind to me.

Then, all the novels said
That if my lover prove
No such man as this
He had to forfeit love.

Now I know life holds
Harder tasks in store.
If my lover fail
I must love him more.

Should he prove unkind,
What am I, that he
Squander soul and strength
Smoothing life for me?

Weak or false or cruel,
Love must still be strong.
All my life I'll learn
How to love as long.

THE SISTERS

They used to say
Our mother brought us up like hot-house flowers,
From day to day
Such wondrous cares were ours
Her love inspired.

In truth we grew
Strangely. Unsought, as priestesses might be.
The girls we knew
Found tenderness. But we
Were more desired.

No doubt at all,
Our spirits drew the secret souls of men.
They would recall
Old dreams through us; and then
Make dreams their choice.

Creatures of light,
Sun-darkened by the shining of her love,
We knew the plight
Of Sibyls, thus to prove
Th' incarnate Voice.

RAIMENT

I cannot be tricked out in lovely clothes
All times, all days.
My mind has moods of hating pearl and rose
And jewel-blaze.

Nor is the body worthily attired
Unless the soul
Has visibly to nobleness aspired
And self-control.

'WHEN I AM ARTICLED'

When I am articled
The Law decrees
I shall devote my time
To stating fees

And learning about Actions,
Suits and Courts.
Then Deeds and Briefs and Grants
Must fill my thoughts.

While if a naughty
Little verse should find
Its way into a corner
Of my mind

I must not tell the chap
For whom I work.
He pays the penalty
If I should shirk

And take to writing books
And verse instead
Of 'hereinafter', 'duly',
'Viz', 'the said'.

I have two loves to learn
The near love and the far love
The love of everyday
And the star love.

Nor dare I yet pronounce
That name compelling.
I-a-v-e-h, E-m-a-n-u-e-l.
I am still spelling.

'I AM NO MYSTIC.
ALL THE WAYS OF GOD'

I am no mystic. All the ways of God
Are dark to me.
I know not if he lived or if he died
In agony.

My every act has reference to man.
Some human need
Of this one, or of that, or of myself
Inspires the deed.

But when I hear the Angelus, I say
A Latin prayer
Hoping the dim incanted words may shine
Some way, somewhere.

Words and a will may work upon my mind
Till ethics turn
To that transcendent mystic love with which
The Seraphim burn.

A PRAYER TO SAINT ROSA

When I am so worn out I cannot sleep
And yet I know I have to work next day
Or lose my job, I sometimes have recourse
To one long dead, who listens when I pray.

I ask Saint Rose of Lima for the sleep
She went without, three hundred years ago
When, lying on thorns and heaps of broken sherd,
She talked with God and made a heaven so.

Then speedily that most compassionate saint
Comes with her gift of deep oblivious hours—
Treasured for centuries in nocturnal space
And heavy with the scent of Lima's flowers.

Text Classics

textclassics.com.au